D0833707

Hunting

Jumping a stone wall.

A PONY CLUB PUBLICATION

Hunting

THE BRITISH HORSE SOCIETY
and THE PONY CLUB

British Library Cataloguing in Publication Data

Jackson, Alastair
    Hunting.
    1. Hunting
    I. Title
    799.2

    ISBN 0-900226-34-X

Designed and produced for The British Horse
Society and The Pony Club by
Threshold Books Limited
661 Fulham Road, London SW6 5PZ

Photographs by Jim Meads
Text by Alastair Jackson

Printed and bound in Great Britain by
Hollen Street Press Ltd, Slough

Contents

Pony Club members watching and listening by a covert.

Introduction

Foxhunting nowadays is flourishing on a greater scale than ever before, with more people participating in it than at any time in its history, and with the spirit of goodwill in the countryside as strong as it ever was. Many of you will find that going out hunting opens up new vistas of enjoyment for both you and your pony. You will be able to put into practice many of the skills of horsemanship that you have already been taught in the Pony Club and elsewhere. You will begin to understand the fascinating art of the huntsman and hounds. And you will have access to parts of the countryside that you would never have a chance to see in other circumstances. Horses and ponies love hunting, so come out and discover for yourself what it is all about!

A well turned-out lady riding side-saddle.

1

The Sport of Foxhunting

Some of you will have been brought up with hunting almost from the cradle – but very many more of you will be new to the sport, and it is to you that this book is principally directed. We hope that it will help you to understand and to gain even more enjoyment from this great country pursuit. Some people who have not been hunting before may be put off by talk of the right clothes and the correct etiquette. This book will try to provide guidance on the clothes and kit which are most practical for the hunting field, and will explain that 'etiquette' is nothing more than normal good manners and respect for the land over which you are riding.

The most important point to remember about foxhunting is that it depends on the goodwill of farmers and landowners. The fact that hounds, staff and followers are welcomed over the privately-owned countryside never ceases to amaze townspeople, but foxhunting is a deep-rooted part of rural life that is inextricably woven into the British country scene. Foxhunting is far from being merely a form of fox control (which it happens to achieve most effectively and humanely – keeping a healthy fox population at acceptable levels). It is a sport enjoyed by thousands of people from many walks of life and is responsible for much of the social life of the countryside at all levels. It plays an important role in conservation, preserving grassland, hedgerows and coverts. It is responsible for a significant amount of employment. And to very many people it can claim to be a way of life as well as a sport.

The development of many equestrian sports stems from

Hounds going to draw in the Midlands.

Hunting on foot in North Wales where the country is too rough and too steep for horses. Note the 'rough-coated' Welsh foxhounds.

the hunting field. Steeplechasing originated from hunting 'thrusters' who would lay wagers against each other to race across country from one church steeple to another. National Hunt racing was evolved from this, and the present-day sport of point-to-point racing is organised by individual Hunts. Show jumping's links with hunting are demonstrated by the red coats worn by riders at major competitions, and by the obstacles – such as the wall, the brush fence, the stile and the oxer – which are based on those found in the hunting field. The cross-country phase of the modern combined train-

Foxhunting in the Lake District. These Fell foxhounds are followed on foot due to the mountainous terrain.

ing (eventing) competition is a natural development from the hunting field and also includes many obstacles to be found out hunting. The relatively new sport of team chasing (racing across country in teams of four) is not only held over hunting country but is organised by the Hunts themselves and administered by the Masters of Foxhounds Association. With the large reserve of horses bred for the hunting field and with horses and riders gaining valuable experience out hunting it is not surprising that equestrian teams from the British Isles are consistently at the top of international competitions.

Hounds hunting in woodland country.

Foxhunting as we know it today is not as old a sport as might be imagined. Though foxes were indeed hunted with hounds many years ago, this was merely regarded as a method of killing a pest. Hounds would meet at daybreak and would hunt the overnight 'drag' of the fox, slowly back to his earth, where he would be dug out and killed. It was the pursuit of the deer that dominated the sporting scene from the time of William the Conqueror – who first introduced organised hunting to the British Isles – to the 18th century.

In 1762 the 5th Duke of Beaufort experienced a thrilling hunt on a fox after an unsuccessful day's stag hunting, and from that day on he decided to teach his hounds to hunt foxes instead. At this period the countryside was being gradually enclosed with hedges and fences, and the sporting squires of Leicestershire discovered the thrill and challenge of riding to hounds by jumping obstacles in their path.

Foxhunting became more and more popular, despite the problems caused by barbed wire, canals, railways, and, not least, two World Wars. It was said of each of these setbacks

Foxhunters out on foot when conditions were unfit for horses.

A pack of beagles moving off from the Meet to hunt hares.

Mr Ben Hardaway III hunting his Midland foxhounds in the Deep
South of the United States of America.

that they would cause an end to hunting, but they certainly
did not. Between the two wars several superb huntsmen
and Royal patronage made hunting in the 'shire' countries
even more glamorous. King Edward VII had always been a
keen hunting man and King Edward VIII and his brothers
all hunted in the Shires.

After the Second World War riding became an
increasingly popular sport, enjoyed by many families who

The Brandywine Hunt in the United States.

had neither equestrian nor country backgrounds. Much of this popularity was due to the development of the Pony Club, which was founded in 1929 and is now one of the largest youth movements in the world. As more and more people took to riding, many of them wanted to experience the thrills of following hounds and the access to the countryside that it gave them.

In recent times the Royal Family have renewed their interest in foxhunting. The Prince of Wales, encouraged by The Princess Royal, made his debut in the hunting field with the Duke of Beaufort's hounds in 1975 and is now a regular and devoted foxhunter. Another happy development since the war has been the introduction and growth of the Hunt Supporters' Clubs, many of whose members follow hounds by car or on foot and bring valuable financial and promotional help to their local Hunts.

There are many forms of hunting around the world, the main quarry being deer, fox and hare. Red deer are hunted

World Champion Three-Day Event horse Priceless out hunting with the Pytchley.

on the moors of the West Country, and the large and healthy herds of deer to be found there are due in no small way to the guardianship of the stag hunts and the popularity that they enjoy with the farmers. Hares are hunted on foot with beagles or basset hounds, and a great deal can be learned and enjoyed from the work of hounds when they are hunting this wily quarry. A slightly larger type of hound is the harrier, which also hunts hares or foxes, but harrier packs are followed on horseback. Foxhounds are sometimes followed on foot, as in the mountains of the Lake District where it would be totally impractical to ride a horse. On the Continent of Europe, where the scourge of rabies has decimated the fox population, there are very many stag hunts.

All over the world, wherever Britons have colonised and settled, they have taken hounds with them: their quarry varying from coyote in North America to jackal in India. In the United States and Canada, where foxhunting continues to flourish, there are no fewer than 150 packs of foxhounds. As would be expected in so vast an area, the type of sport differs enormously. In parts of Canada the freezing climate restricts the season to three or four months, whereas in Georgia and Alabama in the USA's Deep South, hounds are followed in shirt sleeves because of the intense heat. The best foxhunting country in the United States is considered to be in Virginia where the open grassland and timber fences are a delight to ride over.

Even within the British Isles the type of country can vary considerably. The best for riding is still considered to be in Leicestershire where large fields of horsemen can be accommodated and where they can gallop on grass most of the day, spreading out over a wide area to jump the inviting hedges and ditches.

There are many other very much less 'smart' countries offering a great deal of fun. They can vary from the plough countries of East Anglia, the deep woodlands of Sussex and Surrey, and the small fields and banks of Devon and Cornwall, to the wild open hills of the Scottish Borders. In some countries the obstacles will be stone walls, in others they will be mostly timber or hedges. There may be no jumping at all: but there is just as much skill in riding across one of these areas, such as the steep and wild terrain of Exmoor, as in a jumping country. Wherever you hunt, the main ingredients of the sport are the hounds and the fox, and your enjoyment will be greatly enhanced by learning more about the work of the hounds, about the way in which a day's hunting is organised, and about what goes on behind the scenes at the stables and the kennels.

Right Hunting in Leicestershire. A thorn hedge with a ditch towards.

Hunting by a loch in Scotland.

Hounds going to draw a gorse covert in Ireland.

Right, above Hunting in the hills on the Scottish Borders – the wide open spaces of the Cheviots.

Right A pack of foxhounds in Wales passing a derelict coal-mine.

Above Fox cubs at play. *Below* A huntsman casting his hounds.

2

How a Hunt is Organised

The Committee

A Hunt is run very much like a business, with a Chairman, a Board of Directors, known as the Committee, and a Managing Director, who is the Master. The Chairman and his Committee, who are selected from local farmers, landowners and hunting people, are responsible for choosing the Master to run their country and for raising the money to enable him to do so. This is achieved through the subscriptions and caps paid by followers of the Hunt, and by many other functions

The Joint Masters of the Quorn Hunt.

The professional huntsman of the Vale of Aylesbury.

The Hunt Secretary collecting the 'cap' at the Meet.

such as point-to-points, dances, shows and hunter trials. While the Master is in office he supervises the running of the country and the employment of staff. It usually costs him more than the Committee can afford, and in many cases there will be Joint Masters to help with the organisation and the costs.

The Secretary
The Hunt Secretary acts for the Committee in collecting subscriptions, field money and caps from followers. He often also acts as Treasurer. In most Hunts there are special subscription rates and caps for Pony Club members. A cap is the amount that you pay for a day's hunting if you do not already subscribe. The Hunt Secretary (or the Pony Club DC) will tell you how much this is, and it is a great help to the Secretary if you have the correct amount of money with you and give it to him personally. Don't wait for him to find you!

31

A Master who hunts his own hounds. The author with the
Cattistock foxhounds on a wet day.

The Master

While he is in office, the Master is in charge of the stables,
the kennels and the staff. He is responsible for the management of hounds and their breeding, and if he hunts them
himself he will employ a kennel-huntsman to look after the
day-to-day management of the kennels and to whip-in to him
on hunting days. He may employ a professional huntsman,
who will supervise the kennels, and probably a professional
whipper-in, who will also work in the kennels. The Master
has to find horses for himself and for the hunt staff. He also
manages the stables.

Buying horses for a huntsman and whipper-in is a very
costly business these days and is one of the major financial
outlays for a Master. The stable staff have a responsible job
in looking after such valuable animals and keeping them
sound and ready to take their turn on hunting days. The

Master will also probably have to find a lorry to transport the horses and hounds, and a vehicle for the kennel staff to collect carcasses from the farms to feed the hounds. One of the most vital services of the Hunt to the farmer is the prompt collection of any farm animals which die.

Perhaps the most important part of the Master's job is liaising with the local farmers and making sure that the Hunt is welcome on their land. This can be a very time-consuming task, as in most hunting countries there are several hundred farms. Each farmer is likely to have certain requirements – such as the route that followers take, or a certain time of year when he does not want hounds on his land. The Master must discover all these facts and bear them in mind when arranging his meets. There are also other interests in the countryside to be taken into consideration – such as organised pheasant shoots. The keepers and shoot managers must be visited so that shooting dates can be noted before meets are arranged.

Joint Masters thanking farmers for allowing hounds on their land.

The country has to be kept rideable, and this usually means the building of gates, bridges and jumps where necessary. Woodland rides and lanes must also be trimmed so that they are accessible to horses and riders.

It is vital to be able to find foxes on a hunting day, so the management of coverts is most important. Foxes like thick bushes, brambles or gorse to lie in: so when coverts grow too tall and draughty, certain areas have to be 'laid' so that they will grow up thick again. Most Hunts have a covert-laying programme which is carried out every spring.

Finally, the Master is responsible for the organisation of each day's hunting. When he has decided on the direction in which hounds will draw he sends 'warning' cards to notify farmers, earthstoppers and keepers. If the Master is hunting hounds himself, he will brief the Field Master with

Left Hunt gate-shutters at work.

Below Hunt supporters at a Meet in Wales.

Car followers out with the Quorn.

his plans for the day. If a huntsman is employed, he will also be briefed. On the hunting day it is the huntsman with his hounds who has to make the most of the conditions, in order to provide the best possible sport.

The Field Master is often also a Master of Foxhounds, though not necessarily so. It is his job to lead the field (as the followers are called) in such a way that they can see the huntsman and his hounds working, and can enjoy the most entertaining route possible across country, while at the same time avoiding damage to the land and being careful not to interfere with the work of hounds. This is often an exacting task, and the poor Field Master often comes in for a good deal of criticism. It is well nigh impossible to please everyone!

The Supporters' Club
Most Hunts nowadays have a Supporters' Club. This is an organisation based principally on 'foot followers' who enjoy travelling to watch hounds by car, bicycle, or on foot. They are thus able to do their bit to help the Hunt both financially and otherwise. The Club organises all manner of functions, from dances and whist drives to treasure hunts and raffles. As well as raising valuable funds, they also involve a wide cross-section of people in their social life who are not directly involved with hunting. The value of spreading interest in hunting throughout the neighbouring towns and villages is immense.

3

Behind the Scenes

The Kennels and Kennelmen
A professional huntsman is employed to run the kennels unless the Master hunts hounds himself – in which case there will be a kennel-huntsman and in some cases a whipper-in and a kennelman. Large establishments employ up to four men, whereas many of the smaller kennels are run single-handed.

Routine begins early in the morning, when the kennels are meticulously washed down and the bedding for the

Hounds being walked out from the kennels.

hounds is changed as necessary. Hounds will be walked out at least twice a day and will be taken for longer exercise at certain times of the year.

Throughout the day a vehicle is busy picking up dead stock from the farms, and all these animals have to be skinned and prepared for the hounds to eat. It is demanding and unpleasant work for the men concerned, but it is an important service to the farmers, who would otherwise have to bury the corpses.

There will be sick hounds and hounds with injuries to attend to, and bitches with whelps to look after. The huntsman may also have to visit farmers and puppies out

Right The Whipper-in cleaning boots at the Grafton kennels.

Right, below The Kennelman changing the straw on the hound beds.

Below Hounds being fed after hunting at the kennels.

Exercising hounds on bicycles. The Grafton foxhounds near their kennels in Northamptonshire.

at walk. This busy life at the kennels continues all the year round, not just during the hunting season.

Hounds are fed every day: sometimes on raw meat and sometimes on cooked meat mixed with cereal. Feeding generally takes place in the morning, except on hunting days, when hounds are fed on their return to kennels. The huntsman calls them in by name, as some are shy feeders and some eat quickly. With this method he ensures that all hounds are given the correct amount of food.

When the hunting season is over in the spring, hounds are usually allowed to relax for a few weeks and are walked out of the kennels twice a day. However, it is not long before they have to start getting fit again.

Because of the cost of keeping horses up in the summer, early exercise is usually carried out nowadays on bicycles. This enables the huntsman to go further and faster than he can on foot. A few weeks before autumn hunting begins,

The Kennelman walking out the hounds at Badminton.

hounds are exercised from horseback, often for several hours a day. Exercise is not only a method of getting hounds fit; it also plays an important part in the education of young hounds – familiarising them with the country, people, and traffic, as well as with domestic and farm animals.

The Hounds

A few Hunts, such as the Belvoir and the Brocklesby, still breed the pure Old English type of hound, who are mostly dark in colour and are particularly tough.

Most kennels have the 'Modern Foxhound' who was originally evolved from crossing the Old English with the Welsh. The best of these hounds combine great quality and fox sense with the stamina needed for long days in the field.

The Welsh hounds are rough coated and have wonderful noses and voices for hunting in their wild countries. The Fell

A good example of a 'modern' foxhound.

An 'Old English' type of foxhound from the Belvoir.
A Champion Welsh foxhound.

foxhounds have great agility and independence for hunting their foxes unaided high up on the mountains.

Hound breeders – usually Masters – go to an enormous amount of trouble in the breeding of a pack. Pedigrees are studied, as are conformation and nose, voice, and performance in the field.

Puppies are usually born in spring and early summer and are weaned from their mothers at six or eight weeks. They are then ready to go 'out to walk': which means that they are sent out to private homes, where they will live with the family until they are fully grown and ready to go back to the kennels some time during the following winter. During this period they enjoy their freedom, and develop their characters in a way that would not be possible in the kennels.

During the following summer the Puppy Show is held:

A Fell foxhound.

A bitch with her whelps.

Foxhound whelps at about six weeks old.

Puppies being collected by their 'walkers' from the kennels.

often at the kennels, where the young hounds are judged against each other for conformation, and prizes are given to their puppy walkers. This is followed by tea, and is a great social gathering of hunting people in the summer months. It is an opportunity for Masters to say thank you to the puppy walkers and to many other people who have helped them during the previous season.

Some Hunts also show their hounds against each other at various hound shows around the country. There are classes for 'unentered' hounds (young animals who have not yet started hunting), couples, two couples, brood bitches, and stallion hounds. Each region has a hound show, and the premier event is held at Peterborough. Winning a championship here is the highest accolade that a kennel can achieve.

The Duke of Beaufort's Hunt Puppy Show.

The Stables

The Master employs a head groom, sometimes known as the Stud Groom, to run the stables. A large Hunt may stable over twenty horses; a small establishment may have only two or three. One groom – many of them nowadays are girls – will generally look after three or four horses. If autumn hunting is to begin early in September, the horses will be brought in from grass about six weeks beforehand. They will be fat and soft, so it is important for them to be given several weeks' walking on the roads to harden their legs.

At the end of this period, hound exercise – at a slow trot or 'hound jog' – is ideal for the horses. Autumn is a difficult season for the stable staff, as hounds meet at a very early hour, several days a week. The meets become progressively later until the Opening Meet, which is traditionally held in the first week in November.

Once horses are hunting regularly they do not need the same amount of exercise between times, though some horses will always need fast work the day before hunting to clear their wind.

There is also a great deal of clipping to be done before Christmas, which adds to the workload. If the hunt staff have second horses, much of the grooms' hunting day will be spent out of the stables, taking the second horses on. Hunting evenings always finish at a late hour, as there are dirty tack and muddy horses to deal with.

At the end of the season, the horses are roughed off and turned out to grass as soon as the weather is suitable. The head groom usually has a permanent position in most Hunt stables; other grooms are often employed seasonally. However, summer in the stables is relatively short, with horses coming in again in July, and there is plenty to do during the couple of months in which the stables are empty.

Hunt Horses

A hunt horse has to carry the huntsman or whipper-in throughout the long season from August to April. He must

A well-kept stable yard.

be very sound, with powers of endurance, some speed, and a bold jump. Most horses will gallop and jump with the crowd, but the hunt horses must be in front, often turning away from the field to jump a fence with very little stride, sometimes with hounds around his feet. His temperament is also important: he must stand still when necessary and must not mind young hounds bumping his legs and even jumping up against him. Some hunts will keep a cob or two to start hound exercise and for some autumn hunting. This saves

A hunt horse.

Exercising hunt horses in the snow.

the most valuable horses from the wear and tear caused by hunting on hard ground in the autumn.

Long, slow work in the autumn is the secret of getting hunters fit. If you are lucky enough to have hills to work them on, it will pay dividends. Horses turned out in the summer on a hill come in much harder than those turned out in a flat field.

It is always sensible to feed good-quality food, especially hay: the best hay keeps horses clean-winded and economises on the amount of hard food needed. Most hunt stables feed a hot bran mash after hunting.

Hunters should be clipped regularly from October until

January, thereafter only the cat hairs should be trimmed off. A horse who is regularly clipped is easier to keep clean – but this does not mean that time can be saved on grooming, which is also important for toning up the muscles.

In many Hunt stables nowadays horses are hosed after hunting, but great care has to be taken to avoid mud fever and cracked heels. The use of antiseptic wash helps, and heat lamps for the horses to stand under afterwards will dry them off quickly. The head groom must have a good knowledge of veterinary care. Minor wounds and cuts can always be dealt with by staff, and tendon and leg problems can often be avoided by an observant groom, and the necessary precautions can be taken.

Hunt horses should always be shod with studs or road nails all round. Hunt staff inevitably have to gallop on roads and hard surfaces during the course of their duties and their horses must be shod accordingly.

Preparing a hunt horse for a day's hunting.

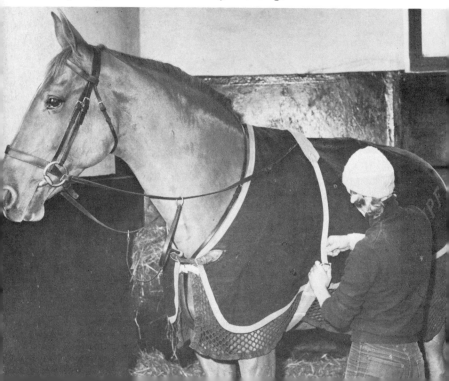

The terrier man with two of his Jack Russell terriers.

The Terrier Man

Most of the larger Hunts employ a professional terrier man and fencing man. In some cases the same person does both jobs, and in many smaller Hunts the duties are undertaken by amateurs and volunteers.

So that foxes can be found above ground on a hunting day, and so that they do not go straight to ground when hunted, it is important to have a system of earthstopping. As farm staff are invariably busy and no longer have the time to undertake this work, more often than not the Hunt terrier man now carries out a great deal of the earthstopping himself.

When a fox is run to ground, a decision has to be made about what to do with him. Often he is left there, but sometimes it is decided to bolt him. In this case, the hounds are taken well away, and a terrier is sent into the earth to encourage the fox to leave so that he may be hunted again. If, on the other hand, the farmer wants the fox to be killed, a terrier is sent into the earth to find him. He is then dug out and shot with a humane killer.

Many Hunts organise an earthstoppers' supper to say thank you to all the local people who help with this important task.

The Fencer

The Hunt fencer has two roles: first to put right any broken fences on a hunting day, and secondly to make the country more rideable by building new jumps, wicket gates, and bridges. With the increase in wire fences, artificial Hunt jumps are now a feature in most countries. If they are strongly built, they have the advantage of not breaking easily. They also encourage followers to use a route with which the farmer is happy. Much of this work can be done in the summer before autumn hunting starts. There will also

Right, above The Hunt fence mender with his vehicle.

Right A fine example of a cut and laid hedge.

An artificial hunt fence. Pytchley Hunt followers in action.

Behind the Scenes

be rides to trim out in the coverts, to enable the hunt staff to get about, as well as gates and jumps to clear.

It is also the fencer's job to 'lay' coverts in the early spring. This consists of cutting and laying chosen areas of thorn and rough covert within a wood. The undergrowth will then become much thicker, with brambles, etc., and will be a much more attractive place for foxes to lie in. Hounds will then be more likely to find them on a hunting day.

A 'mixed' pack of foxhounds.

4

Autumn Hunting

The term 'cubhunting' is misleading in that by the autumn the foxes are fully grown and it takes an expert to tell the difference between a 'cub' and an adult – so in this book we will more accurately refer to *autumn hunting*. It starts as soon as most of the corn has been harvested, and is the 'dress rehearsal' for the main season. At the beginning of the autumn, hounds meet at an early hour (around 7 am) in order to catch the best scenting conditions. Scent tends to lose strength as the day gets warmer. As the autumn progresses and the days become cooler, so the meets are held later.

During these weeks of September and October the huntsman educates his young hounds and discovers the location of foxes. He visits as many parts of his country as he can before the Opening Meet. He also finds out the position of new earths, and decides where a new jump or gate may be needed before the season starts. At this time of year it is important to cull the fox population and to disturb the coverts where they live. Later in the season the huntsman will want to hunt his fox in open country, and if a covert has been properly 'cubhunted' foxes will be more likely to go away quickly when hounds draw it again.

It is normal practice to 'hold up' a covert for a while, in order to ensure that it is thoroughly disturbed and that all the foxes are found. If hounds are allowed to hunt the first fox away, the huntsman will not know if there are more foxes 'at home'.

The Master will tell you if he wants you to help 'hold up' by standing round the covert and tapping your saddle with

Autumn hunting on a misty morning.

your whip. Stand well away from the covert so that you can see a fox if he comes out. Then you can turn him back and shout: 'Tally-Ho Back!'.

The older and bolder foxes may well go away, which is fine. The Master will then probably tell you to let them all go and the hounds will be allowed to hunt in the open.

The young hounds will follow the example of their elders; hunting comes naturally to them anyway. Some will start hunting on their first morning, but you will notice others looking slightly confused, or at first unwilling to leave their huntsman.

This is also the time of year in which hounds will learn that they must hunt fox and nothing else. They will see deer and hares and will be taught that these are 'riot' and must be ignored.

Autumn hunting is organised in different ways, depending on the type of country. (For example, it is obviously not a practical proposition to 'hold up' on the wild hillsides of Wales or Northumberland where foxes are found in hundreds of acres of bracken.) It is also a time during which the Master can prepare his hounds and his country for the main season in November.

A huntsman will generally take out between 16½ couples and 21½ couples of hounds on a hunting day. (Hounds are always counted in couples and it is considered correct to take out an odd number.) Sometimes all bitches or all doghounds are hunted together, but more often they are hunted as a 'mixed' pack. Most hounds are hunted twice a week, but bitches 'in season' and with whelps are kept in kennels, as are a reserve of other hounds to take the place of any who go lame.

5

The Main Hunting Season

The Opening Meet
The Opening Meet takes place in a well-known village or at
a crossroads where there is suitable space for the followers
to collect without disrupting local traffic. The meet may be
held, by invitation, at a private house or farm, and the
Master will allow time for spectators and followers to see
the hounds and their friends before moving off. The Opening
Meet and the Boxing Day Meet are generally very popular
local occasions.

A professional huntsman with his hounds.

A Joint Meet at Badminton House.

Hunting Hounds

Before putting hounds into the first covert, the huntsman will send his whipper-in, and maybe one or two helpers, to position themselves so that they can see a fox go away, but will not head him back. The Field Master and followers are kept out of the way, and the Field Master may well send on a 'link man' who can let him know when hounds have gone away.

A pack of hounds is made up of individuals, all with their own characteristics which will be known by their huntsman. It is fascinating to watch the rapport between a huntsman and his pack and to see how this collection of hounds is welded together to form an effective hunting unit. The whipper-in will help the huntsman with the handling of the hounds and by watching for foxes. He will count the hounds at every opportunity, to make sure that they are 'all on', and will tell the huntsman if any are missing.

A great deal of the success of the day will depend on the scenting conditions. On some days, hounds will find it difficult to smell a fox at all, and on others they will 'fly' from start to finish, needing little help from their huntsman. The best signs for a good scent are when the hedges stand out black, and distant sounds carry clearly. Unsettled weather and warm days are bad for scent.

To begin with, the huntsman will encourage his pack to draw in covert until the first hound speaks and the rest join in. When the fox leaves covert and is viewed away, the whipper-in will wait until the fox is well clear of him. Then he will 'holloa' – an exciting high-pitched yell – to let the huntsman know that the fox has gone. Some hunts use whistles instead of holloaing, as it is less likely to distract hounds.

When hounds are running in the open, the huntsman blows the 'gone away' as a signal to the field that they have left covert. The 'gone away' is a thrilling and easily recognisable call on the horn, to tell the followers that hounds are gone. Other calls on the horn are for the hounds,

Hounds being unboxed at the start of the day.

The Field Master controlling the followers.

Welsh foxhounds about to draw a covert.

Hounds in full cry on the scent of a fox.

The hunted fox.

The Whipper-in bringing on hounds that have been left behind
(tail hounds).

such as the quick staccato notes of 'doubling the horn', to which the hounds should fly when their huntsman needs them in a hurry. When he calls hounds out of a blank covert or is collecting them at the end of the day, he blows a longer, mournful note. He encourages and controls his hounds in a musical voice and a 'defined language', handed down over generations. Much of it was introduced by the Normans in the 11th century.

Sooner or later, depending on the scenting conditions, hounds will come to a check, which means that they have lost the scent of the fox. The huntsman then leaves them alone and watches them fan round in a circle, with their noses down, looking for the line. Nine times out of ten, one or two hounds will 'hit off the line' and will 'give tongue', setting off in the right direction, with the rest of the pack joining in. If hounds cannot work it out for themselves, the huntsman will have to help them. He will try to find out what has caused the check. It may be a 'foil' from sheep or cattle, which has obliterated the scent; or the field may recently have been spread with muck; or perhaps the fox has run up a road (leaving very little scent), or he may have been 'headed' by a vehicle. Having solved several of these problems between them, hounds and huntsman will either lose their fox or will kill him or mark him to ground.

The quality of the sport will depend on how hounds have worked, on the distance covered, and on the particular 'point' made. The point is the distance measured between the two furthest places on the route taken by the fox. A long, circular hunt will not provide the same 'point' as that of a straight hunt – though the distances might be the same. On some days there will be several fast runs; on other days, when the scent is not as good, the runs may be slower. No two days are ever the same – and this is the challenge of foxhunting.

6

Preparation and Turnout

Lack of preparation before a day's hunting can bring discomfort and disappointment: causing you to arrive late at the meet and not being able to find hounds, for example; or to lose a shoe at the beginning of the day.

The day before hunting it is important to check that your pony is fit, well shod, and ready at hand for the morning. If it is possible to keep a grass-kept pony in the night before, you will be saved a lot of work tidying him up. Check that your tack is clean and safe. As ponies often get excited out hunting, causing them to pull much harder than they would normally, a stronger bit may be needed.

If you can, use rubber-covered reins, which are much easier to grip, especially in wet weather on a sweaty pony.

Flashy items of tack – such as coloured browbands or sheepskin nosebands – have no place in the hunting field.

Girth buckles should be checked for wear. Stirrup irons should be large enough not to catch the foot. A numnah is useful to prevent chafing on a fat pony during a long day; the dark-coloured, linen-lined variety are easier to keep clean.

A plaited pony looks smart, but this is not essential, as long as the mane is neatly pulled and the tail is banged at a reasonable length.

Check the amount of time that you will need to set off in the morning in order to arrive at least five minutes before the advertised hour of the meet. Allow plenty of time beforehand to get your pony ready and to have breakfast. Don't forget to take some sandwiches and/or a chocolate bar.

7

Correct Dress

☐ Pony Club members should wear a BSI 4472 crash hat with a dark blue or black cover, or a well-fitted hunting cap with safety harness. The hat should be worn straight, and girls should make sure that they have no hair showing at the front of the hat and that hair at the back is secured in a net.

☐ A tweed jacket should be worn with a collar and tie or a collarless shirt with a white or dark-spotted hunting tie (otherwise known as a 'stock'). This should be held in place with a plain bar tie pin.

☐ Earrings, however small, should never be worn out hunting, as they can get caught in branches of trees or in your chinstrap, and can cause very nasty injuries to your ears.

☐ Fawn jodhpurs with black or brown jodhpur boots should be worn. Older children can wear fawn breeches and riding boots. The boots, even rubber ones, should be well polished, and spurs should be worn high on the seam of the boot above the heel with the blunt ends pointing downwards.

☐ Gloves which do not become slippery when wet are essential; woollen or string ones are recommended.

☐ A hunting whip with thong and lash is both correct and practical. The thong can be used to prevent hounds from getting under your pony, and the handle is invaluable for opening and shutting gates.

The above dress is correct until you are twenty-one or unless you have been awarded the Hunt button by the Master. Being given the button acknowledges that you are a

Correct hunting turnout for Pony Club members.

member of the Hunt; you can now also wear the Hunt collar (if there is a special one) on your black coat. Full details of hunting dress for adults and children are given in the Pony Club publication, *Correct Dress for Riding*.

8

Travelling to the Meet

☐ Six miles an hour is a good average pace for hacking-on.

☐ When riding on the road, always be well mannered. Thank drivers when they slow down for you, and always be friendly with people working in the countryside.

☐ If you are travelling by lorry or trailer, try to find out where you can park your vehicle *off the road*. It is most important not to hinder other traffic, and also not to block gateways or to damage grass verges.

☐ Do not unbox at the meet. This causes congestion and prevents your pony from settling down.

☐ When you arrive at the meet, say 'Good morning' to the Master and the huntsman, then check that your pony and saddlery are in order.

Young riders hacking to a meet in Mid-Wales.

A hunter being boxed up to go to the Meet.

9

Rules for Riding to Hounds

- When you move off from the meet into the hunting field your object should be to ride to hounds so that you can watch and hear them hunting the fox.
- Never forget that wherever you are hunting you are the guest of the local farmer or landowner, and that you are very lucky indeed to be able to have access to private land.
- Because of modern farming techniques, there may well be special routes across certain farms which have been agreed between the farmer and the Hunt. The Field Master will be well acquainted with these routes, and it is important for you to be alert and to follow any instructions which he gives.
- When hounds are drawing, keep quiet and pay careful attention.
- Do not let your pony upset others by fussing or knocking into them. That is the way to get kicked. If your pony is liable to kick, keep him well out of the way. A pony who *habitually* kicks should not be taken hunting.
- When hounds are running, do not bump or cut in on other riders at gateways or jumps. If your pony should stop at a jump, take him back and let everyone else go before you try again.
- When you are told to keep in single file around the edge of cultivated land – such as corn or young grass – make sure that you keep in tight to the edge. This means round the corners as well! Also, keep your distance, and do not tread on the heels of the horse in front, which can cause a nasty injury.
- Jump off your pony quickly to help open or shut a gate.

Pony Club members following the Field Master around the edge of cultivated land.

The Field in full flight over a big hedge in Dorset.

Rules for Riding to Hounds

- Report any damage, such as a broken fence, to the Master or the Secretary.
- Always pass on the message to shut a gate ('Gate, please') loudly and clearly. If there is no-one immediately behind you, either wait for someone, or shut the gate yourself. Never gallop off and leave someone to shut a gate on their own. Always wait and help.
- Always *ride round* a herd of cattle or a flock of sheep. Never alarm them by galloping through them.
- Always make way quickly for the Master or hunt staff, and let other people know by calling 'Master on the left' or 'Huntsman on the right'. If hounds come past you in a lane or a ride, always turn your pony's head towards them and hold the thong of your hunting whip out to prevent them from getting under the pony's feet. This is important – even if you do not think that your pony will kick.
- Never gallop your pony unnecessarily, he may need energy later. Give him an easy time when climbing uphill or in deep going.
- Do not gallop through deep, muddy gateways. Always slow up and collect your pony, as you could have a nasty fall.
- When possible, say 'Good night' and 'Thank you' to the Master and huntsman before going home.

When following in a car there are several things to remember:
- Do not get ahead of the hounds when they are drawing or hunting. You could head the fox and spoil a hunt.
- If you do see a fox, wait until he is well past you before you holloa. Then you will not head him.
- Always park on the same side of the road as other cars so as not to disrupt traffic.
- Do not block gateways or private drives.
- Always switch off your engine when hounds are close by, to avoid noise and fumes.

Jumping a typical East Anglian ditch.

10

The End of the Day

The Journey Home
The pace at which you ride home or to your box must be governed by the condition of your pony. If you have been trotting it is important to walk the last mile or so to allow him to cool off. Loosening the girth by a hole or two will also help him to relax while walking.

It is a good idea to ride your pony into flood water or a brook which has a safe bottom. Let him wash the mud off his legs and belly and then trot him briskly down the road to dry him off.

Care After Hunting
Washing ponies after hunting is far better left to experts: otherwise there is a risk of chills or mud fever. As long as he has had a good feed, a pony who is kept at grass will be far happier turned out in his field at the end of a day's hunting, rather than fretting in a stable to which he is not accustomed.

The day after hunting, a pony at grass must be caught up and checked over for cuts, thorns, girth galls or injuries of any sort. The remaining mud can be brushed off, and he should be trotted up on a level piece of hard ground to test him for lameness. Provided all is well, turn him out again straight away, giving him his hay and feed as usual.

A stabled pony is better off warmly rugged and bandaged, with the worst of the mud knocked off him. Then he can be thoroughly groomed the next day when the mud is dry. There is no harm in washing his tail, though. A tail caked in mud can be very irritating. Tack should be washed off as soon as possible and should be saddle-soaped the same evening.

Members of the South Pembrokeshire hunt washing off their horses in a river.

Hunting Terms

'All on'	The expression used by a whipper-in to tell the huntsman that all the hounds are present.
Account for	To kill or to mark a fox to ground.
At fault	Hounds are 'at fault' when they lose the scent during a hunt.
Babbler	A hound who speaks when he is not on the line of a fox, misleading the huntsman and other hounds.
Blind	A 'blind' ditch is one covered in summer growth. The country is 'blind' in the autumn.
Blowing away	The exciting call on the horn blown by the huntsman when hounds hunt away from a covert.
Blowing out	A longer, less exuberant note blown by the huntsman to call hounds out of a covert where there is no fox (a 'blank' covert).
Bob-tailed	A fox with little or no brush.
Bolt, to	To drive a fox from an earth or a drain with the use of a terrier.
Brood bitch	A female foxhound used for breeding.
Brush	The fox's tail.
Bye day	An extra day's hunting over and above the normal fixtures.
Bullfinch	A high hedge. The horse has to jump *through* the top half.
Cap	The money collected by the Hunt Secretary from non-members (i.e. 'taking the cap round').
Carry the horn, to	To be a huntsman.

Cast	The hounds 'cast' themselves to recover the scent of the fox at a check. The huntsman casts his hounds to help them to do this.
Check	Hounds 'check' when they lose the scent of the fox. When hounds have checked they have to 'cast'.
Chop, to	To kill a fox before it has time to run.
Clean ground	Land which is free of 'foil' or other distracting smells for the hounds.
Cold line	An old scent.
Cold scenting country	A country which does not carry a scent readily.
Couples	Hounds are always counted in couples: therefore 35 hounds are referred to as 17½ couple. 'Couples' are also the collars linked with metal swivels used in the training of young hounds, which are 'coupled' to an old hound on exercise.
Covert	(Pronounced 'cover'.) An area of woodland or gorse which may hold a fox.
Cry	The noise made by hounds when they are hunting.
Cub	A young fox.
Cubhunting	Autumn hunting before the main season starts.
Double	A fence with a ditch on both sides.
Double, to	The huntsman 'doubles his horn' when he blows a series of quick staccato notes on his horn when he needs the hounds in a hurry.
Draft	Hounds which are given to another pack and are said to be 'drafted'.
Drag	The old scent left by a fox when it returns home after a night's hunting.
Draghunting	The sport of following hounds over a pre-arranged line of fences. The hounds hunt an artificially laid scent. The sport is popular in areas that are too restricted by roads or towns to allow proper hunting.

Hunting Terms

Draw, to	Hounds are 'drawing' when they are looking for a fox. The huntsman will 'draw' a hound from the pack when he calls one hound individually.
Earth	The fox's underground home.
Enter, to	A yound hound is 'entered' when it starts hunting for the first time.
Feather, to	A hound 'feathers' when he is following a faint line. He waves his stern and keeps his nose to the ground, but does not speak.
Field	The mounted followers of the Hunt – excluding the Masters and hunt staff.
Field Master	Either the Master himself or someone he appoints to be in charge of the mounted followers.
Fly fence	A fence which can be cleared from a gallop – as compared to a bank.
Foil	Any smell which tends to obliterate the scent of the fox for the hounds.
Guarantee	The sum of money that the Master receives from the Hunt Committee to help cover the cost of running the Hunt.
Hackles	The hairs that stand up along the ridge of a hound's neck when he is angry.
Head, to	To head a fox is to turn him back from the direction in which he is heading.
Heel	When hounds run 'heel' or 'heel-way' they hunt the line of the fox in the opposite direction to which it was travelling.
Hit the line, to	A hound 'hits the line' when he finds the scent after a check.
Hold up, to	To surround a covert in order to prevent foxes from leaving it.
Holloa	(Pronounced 'holler'.) The shout or yell given by someone to inform the huntsman that they have seen a fox.
Hound jog	The very slow trot used when taking hounds on exercise.

Kennel huntsman	A professional hunt servant who looks after the management of the kennels when the hounds are hunted by an amateur. A professional huntsman is his own kennel-huntsman.
Laid (hedges)	*To lay a hedge* is a skilled job, splitting the main growth of the hedge with a 'hook' and laying it over in a pattern to make a stock-proof fence which is still growing. *To lay a covert* is to apply the same technique as above, over thorn and other bushes, so that brambles and undergrowth spread thickly, forming attractive and safe covert for foxes and other wildlife.
Lark, to	To 'lark' is to jump fences unnecessarily when hounds are not hunting.
Lift, to	A huntsman 'lifts' hounds when he calls them to him and takes them to another place where he thinks the fox has gone.
Line	The scent trail of the hunted fox.
Making the pack	Counting hounds.
Mark, to	Hounds bay at the mouth of an earth or drain, to mark – or indicate – that there is a fox inside.
Mask	A fox's head.
Mixed pack	A pack of doghounds and bitches.
Music	A term for the cry of hounds when they are hunting a fox.
Mute	A hound who does not speak to the line of the fox 'runs mute'. It is a serious fault in a hound.
Open, to	When hounds smell the scent of the fox, they 'open' or give tongue.
Opening meet	The first meet of the main hunting season: traditionally around 1 November.
Over-ride, to	To over-ride hounds is to ride amongst them when they are trying to hunt.
Own the line, to	A hound 'owns the line' when it speaks to the scent of the fox.

Hunting Terms

Pad	A fox's foot.
Point	A point is the furthest distance in a straight line covered during the hunt (e.g: the Berkshire hounds ran for 60 minutes scoring a 4½-mile point, but twice as far as hounds ran).
Rate, to	To rate a hound is to tell him off for some misdemeanour.
Ride	A pathway or route cut through woodland.
Ringing	A ringing fox is one which does not run straight.
Riot	A foxhound 'riots' when he hunts any animal other than a fox, such as a deer or hare.
Scent	The smell given off by the hunted animal.
Skirter	A hound who cuts corners instead of following the exact line of the fox.
Speak, to	To give tongue, or to bay.
Stale line	An old scent.
Stallion hound	A male foxhound used for breeding purposes.
Stern	A hound's tail.
Stub bred	Foxes bred above ground rather than in an earth.
Tail hounds	Hounds following behind the main body of the pack when they are hunting.
Tally-ho	A call to say that the fox has been viewed. 'Tally-ho back' (pronounced 'bike') means that the fox has gone back into the cover. 'Tally-ho over' means that he has crossed a ride in the covert.
Throwing tongue	Hounds throw their tongues when they speak to the line of a fox.
Unentered	A young hound who has not started hunting.
Vixen	A female fox.
Walk, to	To walk a foxhound puppy is to rear it in your own home.
Whelps	Unweaned puppies.
Whipper-in	The huntsman's assistant in the field.

94

Index

Figures in *italics* refer to illustrations

Index